"Isolate yourself from others and focus 100X more on your self-improvement":"

Contents

"Read your goals daily to set yourself apart from 99% of people and become a part of the 1%.".

Preface

All your feelings and emotions go unsaid, your wishes and desires remain unfulfilled. There is no change, no happiness you're living with a burden you didn't choose. But the harsh truth is that not everyone accepts their situation. Living Like a mediocre person is one of life's biggest regrets. Your talents remain hidden from others, and reality Strikes: your biggest ambitions and goals vanish before your eyes due to small hesitations. You're pumping yourself up in the dark, but fear holds you back. Mediocre people often believe they're not good enough for anything, destined to live with regrets and a life full of Sadness. A Lack of confidence convinces you that you're not eligible for that. Many of these people have hidden talents they haven't even tried discover, living like everyone else. The key is, to recognise and develop your talents in the right way. You don't need to wait for the perfect situation. The right time to develop your talent and knowledge is now.

I Hope this Book will provide feel good content and change your thoughts even by just one percent. It will help to reduce your negative thoughts. so, don't be afraid to step out of your comfort zone start to work.

PART ONE

Reasons you're stuck in the Same place.

"Losing yourself means aging before your death. Please control yourself and accept the things that happened in your life".

1) The pain you hide

Creating your own emotions in your mind, struggling with them in your life. People don't understand you, and they break you into multiple perspectives. Try to stay conscious, but they don't care, because your life seems less important to others than it is to you.

The pain you hide, prevents you from living with happiness in your present, and you may feel like you're just passing through life, doing things you don't enjoy.

Now, you understand how you feel inside, but in the opposite, you have a greater future. Control your emotions and try to overcome the depression you're experiencing. Just Smile and move on, because the pain you're going through won't last forever. Accept your situation, try to solve it, and remember that time is passing. Your capacity to handle things will eventually be understood by others, because you're at the beginning of a bigger stage. Take care of yourself and push forward.

Wake up and see how beautiful the world can be. The feeling you have alone is not the end; it's an opportunity to identify yourself and find the options available to you. Are you Struggling with loneliness? Give your full power to it and work hard for your success, which will bring you happiness in the world. Control your pain in front of others, but don't forget to show them your strength.

If someone doesn't value your feelings and ignores you, stop crying, stop regretting, and stop doing things for them. Remove yourself from situations where you're not appreciated. Focus on your own happiness because it lies within you. Don't seek happiness from others; Create it for yourself, and make it last.

"Helping others is good, but hurting yourself for others is not".

Make yourself better by letting go of things that no longer serve you. Develop new habits to free your mind from regret. Today's situation may seem difficult and it's hard to overcome the pain of loss, breakup, or unfulfilled expectations, but stay calm. Trust that, the universe has a greater plan for you. Don't worry everything will work out in a positive way. Keep moving forward with trust in your journey.

"The mind, afraid of losing people,
distances itself from those who love
you".

2) Fear of lasing peoples

Life is full of surprises and unexpected events. If someone truly loves you, they will stay in your life forever. Don't be afraid, and don't trap yourself with overthinking. Most the things you worry about never actually happen. understand the difference between your thoughts and reality. People are not always in the way you imagine them to be, so live freely and let go of your worries.

"Don't be afraid of losing people because their hearts may not think the same way you do."

Don't focus on the mistake you made with people who once mattered to you. Instead, recognise the people who truly value and respect you. The one who care about you will never leave you in any situation. The one who don't respect you, however, will not stay, they only come when they need something and will move on once their needs are met.

Don't waste your time on the wrong people. If someone doesn't value your feelings, don't regret to give them your time. Prove to yourself, that you can move on and focus on what truly matters.

Let your actions speak for you and make others feel the jealousy. When they ignore you, focus on your own growth. The people who truly care about you will notice, while those who don't will fade away. Don't be fear of losing anyone, because no one is meant to travel with you forever. Those who want to stay will stay, and those who don't, will move on. Don't waste your time on the wrong people. Focus on living your life with the people who matter most.

When I was a young girl, around 13 or 14, I often played with my toy, and my mother would tell me to join others because I was playing alone. I replied that, I enjoyed playing an my own. Over time, I gave myself space to understand my creative thinking. I realized that, I am a person who enjoys simple things, which others often appreciate. I used to be afraid of what others would think. Fearing that my knowledge was limited and thought that I couldn't do even simple things. But I came to understand, people don't Judge you for your imperfections. I realized that when you doubt yourself, you create fear and distance from others. So, never let self-doubt to control you, as it only leads to fear and isolation.

"Restart your brain with positive thoughts"

3) Unwanted fear and sadness

Unwanted fears and sadness can cloud our minds, often created by overthinking and letting negative thoughts control our lives. We may not even realize it, but our fears and insecurities are deeply rooted in the subconscious, causing us to struggle with feelings of inadequacy. Instead of focusing on fear, think about your childhood and the times when you felt healthy and carefree.

Remember that fear can waste your time and keep you stuck in a cycle of anxiety. Take a step back and focus on the present. Be the one to make your own decisions, without relying on others for validation. Understand that, there are many people in this world facing bigger challenger than you, and yet they keep moving forward. Be present in your life, let go of the fear of the past or future, and create a vision of your future that fills you with peace and happiness. Whenever fear arises, remind yourself to breathe and let it go. Your mind is powerful use it to shape a positive and fulfilling life.

"Controlling your thoughts is the power to control your life".

Release all your unwanted fear, as holding onto them will only cause your inner turmoil. Let go of what weighs you down and create the future you desire.

Whenever fear arises, change your surroundings and look outside to the beauties around you. Observe the trees, the butterflies, and the freedom of birds soaring in the sky. You have the opportunity to spread your wings and rise above.

Nothing in this world is permanent, and if you afraid to act, remember that, your fears will not pass. Turn the page and write the next chapter of your life, filled with happiness and new opportunities. This too shall pass.

"Stop overthinking because what will Happen, will happen."

4) Hurts -caused by overthinking

Overthinking can hurt, especially for those with kind and sensitive hearts. It can keep you awake at night, dwelling on things that others may not even realize. I am proud to be an overthinker, because often, those who overthink have great, caring hearts. Though overthinking may not always be easy to accept, it shows a deep level of empathy and concern for others. Overthinkers tend to care about people so much, that they worry even when others don't seem to appreciate it.

"Think before you think. What is the purpose"?

Your thoughts may become the enemy in your life because many people don't think in a positive way, which can harm your progress. I believe, I have the ability to overcome this. My skills may be below average, but I value my thoughts and ideas. It is important to give value to your own thought in order to overcome pain.

Don't Overthink too much. Especially about others, as it only causes hurt. Overthinking is a trait that can be hard to change, but you can control it within your mind.

Overthinking often leads to procrastination, making it difficult to take action. It can affect your ability to engage with others in a calm and respectful manner.

When you're constantly focusing on what others will think, it can undermine your sense of self-worth. Remember, nothing is more important than inner peace.
Don't waste energy on people who don't value you. Self- respect should always come before Seeking approval. Control your thoughts, avoid overthinking, and focus on the beauty of your future.

"Stay open to receiving the gifts that life has offer:"

*"Search for the meaning of your life,
where you lost your happiness and
hope".*

5) Searching in the part

Many people are trapped in the past, holding onto the pain and sadness of what they have lost, burdened by their emotions and struggling to move forward. Their past is filled with sorrow, brokenness, and battles with their feelings. They search for happiness but they are losing sight of the present. Nothing can change the past, but time is a priceless gift from God, and we must use it to live in the moment. Stop dwelling on what has happened. What's done is done, and it happened for a reason. Learn from your past experiences, and use them to create a better future.

"Start where you are, and remember where you last your hope"

The pain you focus on from your past holds you back, but the happiness lies in the present moment, which you may not fully experience if you're stuck in the past.

Though you may have lost a lot, value your losses and learn from them.

Wake up and embrace the present with the power - you're the only one with the power to change your inner struggles and shape the life as you wish. Make yourself better, add colour to your life and be the person who never gives up. Try to live in the present.

PART TWO

Reasons you haven't Accomplished.
Things at the right time.

"Think before you speak" Is it the right time to say that? Will anything good come from it?

6) Be aware of your words.

Many people often speak without thinking, agreeing to things one moment and changing their minds the next. This inconsistency can create confusion, burdens, and complications in relationships. It's important to be cautious with the words you speak in front of others. There are moments when it's crucial to think before responding.

Why is this important?

When they speak carelessly, we risk causing harm or misunderstanding. Our words have the power to either build or break relationships. This is why communication must be meaningful and thoughtful. Speaking with intention can positively impact your life, but careless words can hurt others and create unnecessary challenges.

The key is to make your mind stable before speaking. Many failures occur when people speak impulsively, giving promises they don't keep, or saying things they regret later. This is why it's essential to think before responding or committing to something.

If you're constantly moving in circles because of rash words or decisions, it becomes difficult to move forward. Be conscious of what you say, as it shapes your future and the relationships around you.

Once upon a time, there were two Tico friends: Wichl and Franckle. Wichl was a quiet speaker, while Franckle was more outspoken. Their group of friends often gathered, but Wichl didn't always get along with them. One day, as they were all talking, Franckle made some surprising comments about their friendship, saying, "My day is full of business and opportunities."

He also mentioned, "Profit is coming, and we need to decorate Our plans". His friends were curious about Franckle's idea, so they Started listening to his business strategies and made money by putting his ideas into action.

However, Secretly, Wichl was working toward his own goals. In the end, he achieved great success.

"Give importance to inner peace; without a peaceful mind, nothing positive will happen in your life".

7) Process your thoughts

Sometimes, you get lost in your thoughts, not realizing that you're drifting away from the present moment, living in an imagined world and wasting your time. It's okay to think, and even to overthink, but some thoughts are positive while others are negative. Ultimately, thinking is just a way of passing time, yet no one is ready to take action and start working.

"You are getting lost in your thoughts."

Be mindful of your thoughts, as they have the power to shape your life. Sometimes, what you think can cause you pain or regret, especially when you are hurt by someone you care about. Everyone faces challenges, and while some may let their ego take control, it's important to focus on solving problems rather than breaking relationships. Always try to think positively and encourage others to do the same, as positive thoughts can lead to a better, more fulfilling life.

"Make yourself busy to distance your thoughts from you. Don't let your thoughts control you'; instead, become the master of your thoughts".

"You can't get your time back So, try to live in the present. Don't regret your past or worry about your future"

8) Stop overthinking for a long time

Stop overthinking and start taking action. Many people spend too much time in thinking about the future and never actually start working towards their goals. Waiting and thinking without action won't bring success. The key is to decide that you will act for your happiness and begin working towards your dreams.

Make progress every day towards your goal. Time is running out, and there are no other options but to start now. The reason some people succeed easily is, that they take action, while others miss their chance because they don't.

Thinking about your goals and your future is important, but success isn't just about thinking; it's about hard work, perseverance, and patience. Focus on doing the work you need to do wait patiently for your dreams to come true.

"Create your own time to present yourself in front of others, as it is

*through these moments, you can improve
and develop your Self-confidence".*

"There's no perfect time in this world; acting with a good heart is always the right time".

9) The right time is Now

Once, when I was a young girl, I went for shopping one day and saw a toy which I really want to buy. I asked my mother, if I could have it, but she told me that we didn't have enough money and we would try again next time. As we left the toy store, I saw a boy on the Street, begging for food. He had no clothes to keep him warm and was shivering in the cold. I felt bad for him and realized that I had been focused on the toy, but this boy had nothing. I didn't ask for anything to him, but I gave him the money and went home.

I couldn't stop thinking about the incident what had happened to that boy? Did he have parents? Why was he begging? it made me realize that everything we have today can be gone tomorrow. I learned that waiting for the perfect time isn't always the answer. The perfect time is now. Don't wait for the future to live your life. Make things happen now, because time changes everything. You might think that today you have nothing, but tomorrow could be different.

"The right time is always the right moment. Don't wait for a perfect time, there is no such thing as a perfect time in this world. Time passes, your age increases. So, there's no time to wait for a perfect moment. Stand up and expose your talent to the world right Now"

Life is a mysterious Journey, and sometimes you may struggle to find your way, as many people waste their time on social media and trivial distractions

Instead of creating happiness, they end up the whole day by scrolling. But why would you choose to live without a purpose without contributing to your own life, or depending on your parents for everything? Time doesn't wait for you whatever you need to do, do it now, for you, hold the key to your own future.

To make yourself stand out from others, you need to differentiate yourself, because people tend to overlook those who are just ordinary. Normal people strive to do things differently from the crowd.

*"Give yourself time to grow and make
yourself proud one day".*

10) Give value to your feelings

Value your feelings because no one else will do it for you. While it's important to think about others, don't forget to prioritise yourself. You often spend so much time focusing on other that you neglect your own well-beings. Your parents are working hard to ensure a better future for you; they are constantly striving, never tiring, just to see a smile on your face and light in your future. Don't waste your time con things or people who don't value you- appreciate those who truly care.

"Stop having others' concerns dumped onto you'; it will hurt you. Give respect to your own existence, and value yourself"

Self-respect is a highest form of esteem within your mind, and you should never let it be diminished by others. It is more important than success because valuing yourself is crucial remember, we are all created uniquely by God.

Don't hurt yourself too much for others; no one is perfect in this world. If you feel down due to your mistakes, take a moment to look at the beauty and variation in the world. Just as, the crow and the peacock are different yet uniquely beautiful, so are we.

"Practice the art of giving happiness and sharing your feelings to help others to improve their lives".

Avoid comparing yourself to others. as it often causes mare pain than physical wounds. Don't dwell on your flaws or imperfections. Instead, search for and embrace your strength and unique qualities, they are beautiful. Ultimately, beauty and perfection are shaped by perception, and everyone sees things differently.

Value your feelings and emotions, don't deceive yourself. It's all about our thoughts and understanding.

*"Create your own path and move forward
on your journey".*

11) Live the way you are living

Don't just copy what others do. If someone creates something, it doesn't mean you should have to do the same. Always be true to yourself and your own path playing someone else's role in life doesn't make you any less of yourself. You should never compare yourself with others, as it leads to self-doubt and shame. Be confident in your own journey and stop trying to live others' lives.

"Don't expect anything from anyone. It's a waste of time. Search within yourself for what you want and be grateful for what you have"

Dare to follow your own ideas and trust that they will let you apart from others. Whatever you passionate about, pursue it build your life the way you want, without comparing it to others. It may feel like something is wrong, but be content with what you have and respect your journey.

*If there's something you wish to do,
go for it and do it the right way. Don't try
to live someone else's life – live your own.*

"Nourish your soul with positive thoughts, as they have the power to heal your mind and transform your life"

12) Nothing hurts more than your thoughts.

Nothing can harm you more than your own thoughts. They have the power to disturb your inner peace, so it's essential to process them carefully. If you make a mistake, work on correcting it instead of overthinking and hurting yourself emotionally. If you make someone upset, don't hesitate to apologize. True friends will accept your apology and support you in correcting your mistakes.

However, if someone doesn't accept your apology, don't dwell on it; it's not worth your energy. Taking responsibility for your actions is important, but not everyone will understand.

Similarly, if someone upsets you remember that " This too shall pass", use the experience to learn and grow stronger. When you fail at something, don't give up, keep moving forward and look for new opportunities. Failure is just a stepping stone to success. Don't let your thoughts trap you in self-doubt. Keep striving and searching for better ideas and paths to achieve your goals.

"Your thoughts are the real enemy. Stop dwelling, won them and just move on. Focus on what you can do to make your life better".

PART THREE

Tips to overcome procrastination

13) Practice self-discipline

Changing your mindset may be tough, especially when you're struggling with procrastination and laziness. It can seem difficult to start working toward your dreams, but it is important to trust that, change is possible. Your sub-conscious mind might be trained to act lazily, but this doesn't mean you can't reprogram it.

A key reason for procrastination and laziness is often rooted in habits formed overtime. However, you have the power to rewire your brain and break free from these patterns. Once you decide to change, don't look back. It's important to forgive your past mistakes and focus on the future you want to create.

Here's a tip to help you overcome procrastination and laziness:

***Step 1:** Go to a shop and buy a small plant. If you already have a favourite plant, that's great too. Put the plant on a pot and place it same near where you sleep.*

***Step 2**: Every morning, when you wake up, ask your plant to "wake up" with you. Take the pot outside, let it soak in the sunlight, and gently water it. Sit down and observe the plant. Notice how it grows and thrives, absorbing the sunlight and water.*

***Step 3:** Use this time to reflect on your emotions and thoughts. Allow the plant to become a symbol of your own growth. Let it be a reminder of the changes you wish to make in your life. By caring for the plant every day, you'll start feeling more connected to your intentions, slowly easing any stress or anxiety.*

The goal is to see the plant as part of your journey, symbolizing the changes you're making in your life. By repeating this process, you'll be training yourself to be more mindful and intentional, which can help to overcome procrastination and laziness.

Remember, growth takes time. Be patient with yourself, and stay committed to your goals.

Practice one habit every day. I am not saying you must do meditation, yoga, or exercise. In the beginning, you don't need to commit hours. Just spend 15 minutes every day focusing on your future goals. Whether your dream is to become a doctor, or a businessman, or anything else, dedicate those 15 minutes every day to think about your goals and plans. Instead of wasting time on things that don't matter, use 15 minutes to invest in your career. By doing this every day, you'll see progress. If you can stick with these habits for a week without procrastination, you'll notice the positive changes in yourself. This small commitment can have a big impact on your life and future.

14) Engage in self-talk

Many people try to make an impact on others' lives, forgetting to prioritize themselves in the process. They put all their efforts into impressing someone they like, but the truth is, those people may not even value their words. Too often, people waste their time and emotions on the wrong individuals, unaware that inner peace is more important. The treasure of self-value, understanding, and growth lies within us. Believing in yourself is the biggest key to success.

Start listening to your heart, trust what it tells you, and let your mind explore innovative ideas. Take time to reflect and identify who you truly are. self-talk is a farm of meditation, and giving yourself space is the test of your life. This process can heal your soul, cultivate positive thoughts, and help you to overcome challenges. It allows you to distinguish between right and wrong and discover what makes you happy. Don't listen to other's criticism; work hard for your career and success. Making time for yourself is the first step toward your journey of self-fulfilment.

"Believe in yourself, and you will achieve it."

15) Destroy your distractions

Distractions, like social media, are often seen as the cause of people closing focus on their goals. However, the real issues are emotional and mental distractions, such as laziness and procrastination. These may prevent people from moving forward with their plans and can cause frustration. While social media we may seem like, escaping the core problem lies in not managing your thoughts and emotions.

To overcome these distractions and achieve your goals:
Step:1

1) Understand procrastination:

Procrastination is a habit that destroys productivity. people tend to delay tasks, but often don't notice how much time is wasted on things like mobile use. Instead of Scrolling endlessly, take small action to break this habit.

2) *Make time for yourself:*

If you feel bored, avoid going to your phone. Instead, take a walk, observe nature, or reflect on your future. Spend quality time alone to connect with your purpose.

3) *Face your fears:*

Identify the root causes of your procrastination or confront these fears, and take small but consistent step toward your goal. Every effort count, and over time, you'll begin to see change.

The key to recognize and control your distractions, take action, and Stay committed to your goals.

Step:2

Buy a boak by Horror or Thriller and read one chapter every day. This simple habit will speak your interest and help you focus on important things. Many people live without passion or interest in their lives, but this practice will motivate you to start your day with purpose. As you read chapter by chapter, you'll feel more engaged and inspired to move forward, creating a sense of excitement for the next chapter of your life and encouraging you to take meaningful action.

16) Motivation doesn't work all the time

Motivation can boost your confidence, but it often fades quickly, leaving you feeling drained and potentially leading you to give up. Self-discipline, however, is a key. If you continue pushing yourself even when your brain urges you to stop, you'll build resilience. Many people give up because they listen to that voice telling them to quit, but persistence leads to success. The key to progress is doing the work consistently, even when you don't like it.

Push yourself beyond your comfort zone. The more you do, the more you'll grow. You may discover new strengths which you didn't know that you had.

People with clear goals are the one who succeed. Many work tirelessly thinking that desire alone is enough, but ambition is what drives you to act. Everyone's goals are shaped by their circumstances, but ambition pushes you beyond those boundaries.

Don't let past mistakes or pain define you. Learn from them and take action. Disciplines today, shapes a better tomorrow. Let your past struggles be a fuel that drive to create your future that's different from the one you fear. Understand yourself, and move forward without hesitation.

17) Don't dry to attract people

__"Stop chasing people for attention or validation"__. Trying to fit into a mold or imitate others will only destroy your true self. Be authentic, embrace your natural talents, and express your best version. If people don't value your words or show respect, don't worry about it. Write down your thoughts in a Journal, and focus on your own growth. Be silent when needed; you don't have to explain yourself to everyone. Control your emotions and keep them within. Don't make yourself available for people who don't value you or your dreams. Let your actions speak for themselves, work in silence, and be a mystery to others.

Your respect will increase when you stop trying to attract people. Instead, focus on making yourself and be someone whom drawn to people who truly value you will respect your boundaries.

"Never underestimate yourself, because you may not know the hidden talents within you".

ACKNOWLEDGEMENT

Life is precious gift, and in every chapter, we receive different blessings. One of the greatest gifts in my life is my father. He thought me valuable lessons, supported me unconditionally, and never let me give up on my dreams. I feel truly blessed to have had him by my side.

I also want to express my gratitude to a dear friend who has always there for me. During my toughest times, she inspired me, consoled me, and helped me to refocus on my goals. I feel incredibly lucky to have had her support. She often feels that she wasn't doing enough for me but in reality, she was the only one who truly understood my struggles.

Gratitude is a magical force; it brings warmth to the world when shared with a kind heart. Nowadays, happiness seems elusive for many because they fail to notice the joy that already exists within them. Appreciate what you have instead of dwelling on what is missing.

*"Gratitude – one word that can change
your whole life. The feeling of gratitude
shapes your journey, and when you
embrace it, life moves in the direction
you desire."*

Editor:
divyadharshini9894@gmail.com

www.ingramcontent.com/pod-product-compliance
Lightning Source LLC
Chambersburg PA
CBHW020651160726
47991CB00003B/1136